Groomed for Greatness: The Young Adult's Guide to Personal Wellness

DERICK CHIBILU

Published by Books By Derick Chibilu, 2024.

Groomed for Greatness: The Young Adult's Guide to Personal Wellness

DERICK CHIBILU

Copyright

Book Description

"Groomed for Greatness" is an empowering and comprehensive guide specially crafted for young adults, offering a treasure trove of knowledge on personal hygiene and grooming practices. In this immersive book, young readers will embark on a journey of self-discovery, learning how to maintain their health, appearance, and overall well-being with confidence and grace.

With engaging and informative chapters, "Groomed for Greatness" covers all aspects of personal hygiene, making it a must-have resource for young adults seeking to develop healthy habits that last a lifetime. From mastering the art of daily bathing to understanding the significance of proper dental care, each chapter delves into the importance of these essential practices in enhancing not just appearance but also mental and physical health.

As young adults dive into this empowering guide, they'll explore the secrets of skincare, hair care, nail care, and foot hygiene, discovering how to create a personalized routine that brings out their natural radiance. Empowered with knowledge, they'll also gain insights into addressing specific skin concerns, such as acne and dry skin, and understanding the importance of sun protection in safeguarding their skin from harmful UV rays.

Moreover, "Groomed for Greatness" extends beyond the physical aspects of hygiene, providing valuable guidance on social grooming, including proper handshakes, maintaining eye contact, and basic etiquette in various social situations. Young adults will develop social confidence, making positive impressions in both personal and professional settings.

Addressing topics often considered sensitive or overlooked, this guide also discusses personal odor management, menstrual hygiene for females, and pubic hair grooming for those seeking to learn about these crucial aspects of self-care.

By grasping the significance of overall body wellness, young readers will come to understand that personal hygiene isn't just about appearance—it's a foundation for holistic health and well-being. Each practice mentioned in "Groomed for Greatness" contributes to nurturing their bodies as temples of the Holy Spirit, aligning with Christian principles of self-care, stewardship, and self-respect.

As they implement the knowledge gained from this book into their daily lives, young adults will not only present themselves confidently but also cultivate habits that positively impact their physical and mental health. "Groomed for Greatness" is an empowering companion for young adults on their journey toward self-discovery, personal growth, and the realization of their inherent greatness.

Introduction

Welcome to a transformative journey of self-discovery, empowerment, and personal growth—welcome to "Groomed for Greatness: The Young Adult's Guide to Personal Wellness." In the bustling world of young adulthood, where life presents an array of challenges and opportunities, taking charge of your well-being becomes an invigorating quest. As you turn the pages of this comprehensive guide, you'll unlock the secrets to mastering the art of personal hygiene and grooming, leading you to a path of radiant confidence and inner greatness.

Chapter by chapter, "Groomed for Greatness" offers you an immersive and captivating exploration of the many facets of personal hygiene, creating a holistic approach to nurturing your mind, body, and spirit. We understand that being a young adult is exhilarating yet overwhelming, as you face pivotal moments of change and growth. But fret not, dear reader, for within these pages lie a treasure trove of knowledge and wisdom tailored to suit your unique journey.

In the fast-paced world we live in, it's easy to overlook the importance of self-care. However, "Groomed for Greatness" is not just another mundane guide—it's a dynamic adventure designed to captivate and inspire you. Through relatable stories, illustrations, and engaging content, you'll be drawn into a world where personal wellness becomes a beacon of light, illuminating your path towards greatness.

As we embark on this transformative expedition, we begin with the foundation of personal hygiene—daily bathing and showering. Understanding the significance of keeping your body clean and fresh, you'll discover how this simple, yet profound practice becomes a steppingstone to self-confidence and well-being.

Next, we delve into the realm of oral hygiene—a gateway to a captivating smile and a healthy mouth. Unravel the secrets of proper dental care, learn the art of brushing teeth, flossing, and visiting the dentist regularly. A radiant smile can indeed be the key to brighter days and unforgettable encounters.

Hand hygiene takes center stage as we unravel the significance of washing your hands thoroughly and frequently. A small yet impactful practice, it empowers you to take charge of your health and prevent the spread of germs, a testament to your commitment to safeguarding yourself and those around you.

Nurturing your hair and nails is an art that resonates with self-expression and individuality. Within these chapters, you'll master the secrets of hair care, learning how to keep your locks clean, conditioned, and healthy. As for your nails, discover the joys of keeping them clean, trimmed, and groomed, a reflection of your attention to detail and self-respect.

In "Groomed for Greatness," we embrace the art of grooming facial hair, exploring proper shaving techniques and the uniqueness it adds to your appearance. Embrace your identity and unleash the potential of your facial hair, reflecting your individuality and personal style.

Furthermore, we delve into the essence of deodorant and antiperspirant use, recognizing its role in managing body odor and sweat. Stay fresh and confident throughout the day, understanding that your body is a temple to be cherished and respected.

With each turn of the page, you'll uncover the secrets of caring for your clothes and understanding how to launder and maintain them to radiate cleanliness and elegance.

The journey towards overall body wellness is incomplete without addressing foot hygiene. Delve into the significance of regular washing, proper footwear, and addressing foot-related issues to ensure that each step you take is one towards vibrant well-being.

Being aware of personal odor management and understanding menstrual hygiene practices are essential aspects of self-care. We address these topics with sensitivity and respect, recognizing their significance in your overall health and confidence.

For those seeking guidance on pubic hair grooming and skincare for specific concerns, these chapters provide valuable insights into understanding and nurturing your body with care and love.

Moreover, discover the significance of sun protection in safeguarding your skin from harmful UV rays, unlocking the secrets to preserving youthful radiance and healthy skin.

Beyond the physical, we dive into the realm of social grooming, emphasizing proper handshakes, maintaining eye contact, and mastering basic etiquette in social situations. Empower yourself to create lasting impressions and cultivate genuine connections in all walks of life.

Throughout "Groomed for Greatness," you'll also gain essential knowledge on the proper use of personal care products, recognizing the importance of their appropriate and safe application.

Moreover, caring for personal items becomes a testament to your commitment to hygiene and responsibility, fostering a deeper appreciation for the belongings you cherish.

Lastly, as we celebrate the beauty of diversity, we recognize the significance of understanding body changes during puberty, offering guidance to adapt your hygiene routines accordingly.

With each chapter, "Groomed for Greatness" extends an invitation to embrace your inherent greatness, to honor your body as a temple of the Holy Spirit, and to radiate confidence and well-being. Prepare to embark on an unforgettable journey of self-love, empowerment, and the discovery of the greatness that resides within you. Are you ready to emerge as the best version of yourself? The adventure awaits. Let's begin!

Daily Bathing/Showering: Understanding the Importance of Regular Cleansing

Daily bathing or showering is a crucial aspect of personal hygiene that plays a significant role in keeping the body clean and fresh. This routine practice involves washing the body with water and soap, helping to remove dirt, sweat, oils, and bacteria that accumulate on the skin throughout the day. Beyond the obvious benefits of maintaining cleanliness, daily bathing also promotes overall health, boosts self-confidence, and contributes to a positive outlook on life.

Importance of Regular Bathing/Showering:

Physical Hygiene: Daily bathing is essential for removing surface dirt and germs from the skin. Sweat, oils, and dead skin cells can build up, leading to clogged pores and potential skin issues if not regularly washed away. A clean body reduces the risk of skin infections and helps to maintain healthy skin.

Body Odor Control: Regular bathing effectively controls body odor, which can result from bacterial activity on the skin's surface. The fresh, clean feeling after bathing not only benefits the individual but also makes social interactions more pleasant.

Mental and Emotional Well-being: Bathing or showering has a therapeutic effect on the mind. The act of cleansing can be relaxing and rejuvenating, reducing stress and anxiety. Feeling clean and fresh can boost self-esteem, leading to a more positive outlook on life.

Preventing Illness: Daily bathing helps prevent the spread of germs and reduces the risk of infections and illnesses caused by external factors. It is especially important during cold and flu seasons or when in contact with potentially harmful substances.

Social and Cultural Norms: In many societies, daily bathing is considered a standard practice and part of acceptable personal hygiene. Adhering to these norms demonstrates respect for oneself and others.

Illustrations and Examples:

Consider a scenario where an individual spends a hot summer day outdoors engaging in physical activities. Throughout the day, their skin accumulates sweat, dirt, and sunscreen residue. By the end of the day, their body feels sticky, and they might notice a faint unpleasant odor. Taking a shower before bedtime removes all the accumulated impurities, cools down the body, and prepares them for a comfortable and refreshing night's sleep.

Another example is a person who works in an environment with potential exposure to bacteria or pollutants. Regular daily bathing in the morning and evening ensures that they maintain personal hygiene and minimize the risk of contracting infections or carrying germs to other areas of their life, such as their home or social gatherings.

Application to a Christian Lifestyle as a Young Man:

Incorporating daily bathing into a Christian lifestyle as a young man aligns with the principle of stewardship—caring for the body as a temple of the Holy Spirit (1 Corinthians 6:19-20). Here's how daily bathing connects with Christian values:

Respect for God's Creation: By maintaining personal hygiene, a young man recognizes that his body is a gift from God. Taking care of it through regular cleansing reflects gratitude and respect for the physical vessel provided to fulfill God's purpose.

Modesty and Cleanliness: Christianity emphasizes modesty and cleanliness as a reflection of inner purity. Regular bathing helps a young man present himself in a clean and respectable manner, avoiding any offensive odors that could distract from his message or interactions with others.

Consideration for Others: Practicing daily bathing demonstrates thoughtfulness and consideration for others' comfort. It ensures that a young man doesn't unknowingly become a source of discomfort for those around him due to body odor or uncleanliness.

Discipline and Self-Control: Establishing a routine of daily bathing requires discipline and self-control. As a Christian, cultivating self-discipline is essential in various aspects of life, including personal hygiene.

Gracious Hospitality: When engaging in church activities or serving others, maintaining personal cleanliness contributes to a welcoming and hospitable environment. By presenting himself cleanly, a young man can be more effective in sharing Christ's love with others.

In summary, daily bathing or showering is a fundamental practice that goes beyond mere cleanliness; it encompasses physical well-being, mental refreshment, and respect for oneself and others. For a young man following a Christian lifestyle, regular bathing aligns with biblical principles of stewardship, modesty, consideration for others, and self-discipline. By incorporating this hygienic routine into his daily life, he not only maintains good health but also reflects the values of his faith in practical ways.

Oral Hygiene: Understanding Proper Dental Care for Optimal Health

Oral hygiene is the practice of maintaining clean and healthy teeth and gums to prevent dental issues such as cavities, gum disease, and bad breath. It involves a combination of regular habits, including brushing teeth at least twice daily, flossing, and visiting the dentist for check-ups and cleanings. Good oral hygiene not only promotes a bright and confident smile but also contributes to overall well-being, as poor oral health has been linked to various systemic health conditions.

Proper Dental Care Practices:

Brushing Teeth Twice a Day: Brushing teeth at least twice a day, ideally in the morning and before bedtime, is fundamental to oral hygiene. Using fluoride toothpaste and a soft-bristled toothbrush, one should clean all surfaces of the teeth, including the front, back, and chewing surfaces. Brushing helps remove plaque—a sticky film of bacteria that forms on teeth—which, if left untreated, can lead to tooth decay and gum disease.

Flossing Daily: Flossing is an essential complement to brushing, as it reaches areas between the teeth that a toothbrush cannot effectively clean. Flossing removes food particles and plaque from these tight spaces, reducing the risk of cavities and gum inflammation.

Regular Dental Check-ups: Visiting the dentist for regular check-ups and cleanings is crucial for maintaining oral health. Dentists can identify and address dental issues early on, preventing them from progressing into more serious problems. Professional cleanings also remove tartar—a hardened form of plaque that cannot be removed by brushing alone.

Illustrations and Examples:

Consider a scenario where an individual neglects their oral hygiene. They occasionally brush their teeth irregularly, skip flossing, and rarely visit the dentist. Over time, plaque accumulates on their teeth, leading to the development of cavities and gum inflammation. The lack of professional cleanings allows tartar to build up, causing further gum issues. As a result, the person experiences dental pain, discomfort, and an unsightly smile, which can impact their self-esteem and overall quality of life.

In contrast, someone who follows proper oral hygiene practices consistently brushes their teeth twice a day, flosses diligently, and visits the dentist every six months. They enjoy healthier teeth and gums, fresher breath, and fewer dental problems. Their smile exudes confidence and reflects their commitment to maintaining oral health.

Application to a Christian Lifestyle as a Young Man:

Incorporating proper dental care into a Christian lifestyle as a young man aligns with biblical principles of stewardship, self-discipline, and caring for oneself and others. Here's how it applies:

Stewardship of the Body: As mentioned earlier, the body is considered a temple of the Holy Spirit in Christianity (1 Corinthians 6:19-20). Caring for one's oral health is an act of stewardship, acknowledging that the body is a gift from God and should be maintained in good condition.

Self-Discipline and Responsibility: Practicing good oral hygiene requires self-discipline, as it involves establishing and maintaining a daily routine. As a Christian, developing self-discipline is vital not only for oral health but also for personal and spiritual growth.

Caring for Others: Maintaining proper oral hygiene demonstrates consideration for others. Bad breath and dental issues can negatively impact social interactions and relationships. By taking care of oral health, a young man shows respect for those around him and ensures that his presence is pleasant and welcoming.

Gratitude and Thankfulness: Regular dental care can often be taken for granted, but a young man following a Christian lifestyle can approach oral hygiene with gratitude and thankfulness. He recognizes that not everyone has access to such care and appreciates the opportunity to preserve his oral health.

Wise Stewardship of Resources: Preventive dental care, such as regular check-ups, is a wise use of resources. By addressing dental issues early, a young man avoids more significant expenses and potential discomfort in the future.

In summary, proper oral hygiene is vital for maintaining healthy teeth and gums, promoting overall well-being, and presenting oneself confidently. As a young man living a Christian lifestyle, incorporating regular dental care aligns with principles of stewardship, self-discipline, and consideration for others. By practicing good oral hygiene, he not only preserves his oral health but also reflects his Christian values in practical ways, caring for the body as a temple of the Holy Spirit and demonstrating gratitude for the blessings he has received.

Hand Hygiene: Understanding the Significance of Thorough and Frequent Handwashing

Hand hygiene refers to the practice of washing hands thoroughly and frequently to prevent the spread of germs, bacteria, and viruses that can cause infections and illnesses. It is one of the simplest yet most effective ways to protect oneself and others from various contagious diseases. Regular handwashing is especially critical during times of outbreaks, such as flu seasons or pandemics, as it can significantly reduce the risk of transmission.

Significance of Thorough and Frequent Handwashing:

Preventing Illness: Hands come into contact with numerous surfaces throughout the day, and these surfaces can harbor harmful germs. When people touch their face, mouth, or eyes, they can unknowingly transfer these germs into their bodies, leading to infections. Proper handwashing disrupts this transmission route, reducing the likelihood of getting sick.

Protecting Others: Hand hygiene is not only about safeguarding oneself but also about protecting others. When individuals wash their hands, they reduce the number of germs they may spread to surfaces or when touching objects that others will handle.

Reducing Hospital-Acquired Infections: In healthcare settings, thorough handwashing is critical to preventing the spread of infections between patients, healthcare workers, and visitors. It is a cornerstone of infection control in hospitals and clinics.

Instilling a Healthy Habit: Teaching and practicing good hand hygiene from a young age instills a healthy habit that can last a lifetime. By making handwashing a routine, individuals are more likely to adhere to it even during busy or challenging times.

Emergency Preparedness: During outbreaks or public health emergencies, hand hygiene becomes even more crucial. It can be a simple yet powerful measure to contain the spread of diseases within communities.

Illustrations and Examples:

Consider a situation where a group of friends gathers for a meal at a restaurant. Before eating, they all wash their hands thoroughly with soap and water, ensuring they eliminate any germs they might have picked up during their day. By doing so, they reduce the risk of transferring potential germs to their food and mouth, safeguarding their health and the health of others.

Another example is in a healthcare setting. Nurses, doctors, and other healthcare providers diligently follow hand hygiene protocols, washing their hands before and after patient interactions. This practice prevents the transmission of infections between patients and healthcare workers, ensuring a safer environment for everyone.

Application to a Christian Lifestyle as a Young Man:

Incorporating thorough and frequent handwashing into a Christian lifestyle as a young man aligns with the principles of love, compassion, and caring for others. Here's how it applies:

Love Your Neighbor: Hand hygiene is an act of love for others. By washing hands regularly and thoroughly, a young man shows consideration for the well-being of those around him, protecting them from potential illnesses.

Compassion for the Vulnerable: Some individuals, such as the elderly, young children, or those with compromised immune systems, are more susceptible to infections. Practicing proper hand hygiene helps safeguard the vulnerable members of the community.

Stewardship of the Body: As mentioned earlier, Christians view their bodies as temples of the Holy Spirit. Taking care of one's health through handwashing is a responsible and mindful act of stewardship.

Community Responsibility: As a member of a Christian community, a young man has a responsibility to contribute to the well-being of the community. By practicing good hand hygiene, he actively participates in promoting a healthier environment for all.

Witnessing through Action: In Christianity, actions often speak louder than words. By demonstrating a commitment to hand hygiene, a young man sets an example for others, encouraging them to adopt similar practices and promoting overall community health.

In summary, thorough and frequent handwashing is a simple yet powerful practice that can prevent the spread of germs and protect both oneself and others from illnesses. As a young man following a Christian lifestyle, incorporating this practice aligns with principles of love, compassion, stewardship, and community responsibility. By making hand hygiene a part of his daily routine, he not only cares for his own well-being but also reflects his Christian values through practical acts of consideration and love for others.

Hair Care: Understanding the Importance of Washing, Conditioning, and Maintaining Hair for Clean and Healthy Tresses

Hair care is a crucial aspect of personal grooming that involves various practices to keep hair clean, nourished, and healthy. It encompasses regular washing, conditioning, and other maintenance routines to promote strong, lustrous, and manageable hair. Proper hair care not only enhances one's physical appearance but also contributes to overall self-confidence and well-being.

Importance of Hair Care:

Scalp and Hair Health: Regular hair care, including washing and conditioning, helps maintain a healthy scalp and hair follicles. Clean hair and a nourished scalp promote hair growth, reduce dandruff, and minimize the risk of scalp infections.

Cleanliness and Hygiene: Washing hair regularly removes accumulated dirt, excess oils, and environmental pollutants. Clean hair looks and feels fresh, making it more pleasant for oneself and others.

Preventing Hair Damage: Conditioning hair helps improve its strength and elasticity, reducing the likelihood of breakage and split ends. Proper care can prevent hair from becoming dry, brittle, and prone to damage.

Self-Confidence: Healthy and well-groomed hair enhances self-confidence and self-esteem. Feeling good about one's appearance positively impacts overall emotional well-being.

Professional and Social Interactions: Well-maintained hair can create a positive impression in professional and social settings, contributing to a confident and presentable image.

Hair Care Practices:

Washing: Washing hair with a suitable shampoo cleanses the scalp and hair, removing dirt, oils, and product buildup. The frequency of washing varies based on hair type and individual preferences but is typically done every two to three days.

Conditioning: Applying conditioner after shampooing helps restore moisture to the hair, making it more manageable and reducing tangles. Conditioning also protects hair from damage caused by heat styling and environmental factors.

Trimming: Regular hair trims remove split ends, promoting healthier hair growth and preventing further damage along the hair shaft.

Protective Styling: Using gentle and protective hairstyles, such as braids or buns, can minimize hair breakage and tangling, especially during sleep or physical activities.

Avoiding Harsh Treatments: Limiting the use of heat styling tools, chemical treatments, and excessive hair products helps prevent hair damage and maintain its natural strength and shine.

Illustrations and Examples:

Imagine a young man who diligently follows a hair care routine. He washes his hair every two days, using a mild shampoo to cleanse his scalp and hair thoroughly. After each wash, he applies a nourishing conditioner to keep his hair hydrated and manageable. Every few months, he visits the barber for a trim to remove split ends and maintain a neat appearance. By following these practices, his hair remains healthy, shiny, and well-groomed.

In contrast, consider a scenario where a young man neglects his hair care. He washes his hair irregularly, leading to greasiness and an unkempt appearance. Due to the lack of conditioning, his hair becomes dry and prone to tangles and breakage. Over time, split ends develop, making his hair look frizzy and damaged.

Application to a Christian Lifestyle as a Young Man:

Incorporating proper hair care into a Christian lifestyle aligns with principles of self-respect, stewardship, and presenting oneself in a manner that reflects Christian values. Here's how it applies:

Stewardship of the Body: Taking care of one's hair is an act of stewardship, recognizing that the body is a gift from God. As a young man following a Christian lifestyle, he acknowledges the importance of maintaining his physical appearance as a reflection of gratitude for God's creation.

Respect for Others: Proper hair care contributes to a neat and presentable appearance, showing respect for oneself and consideration for others. A young man who cares for his hair portrays a positive image in his interactions with others, reflecting humility and respect.

Self-Discipline and Responsibility: Establishing a regular hair care routine requires self-discipline and responsibility. A young man can apply the discipline he develops through hair care to other aspects of his life, such as spiritual practices and personal goals.

Modesty and Humility: Proper hair care allows a young man to present himself modestly and humbly, avoiding excessive focus on his appearance. A balanced approach to grooming reflects inner qualities and values over excessive vanity.

Self-Confidence and Service: When a young man feels confident about his appearance, it can positively impact his demeanor and interactions with others. A self-assured attitude can help him serve others with greater assurance and humility.

In summary, hair care is essential for maintaining clean, healthy, and well-groomed hair. As a young man following a Christian lifestyle, incorporating proper hair care aligns with principles of stewardship, respect for oneself and others, self-discipline, and modesty. By taking care of his hair, he not only enhances his physical appearance but also reflects Christian values through the way he presents himself to the world.

Skincare: Understanding the Basics of Cleansing, Moisturizing, and Sun Protection for Healthy and Radiant Skin

Skincare is the practice of maintaining the health and appearance of the skin through various routines and products. It involves essential steps such as cleansing to remove impurities, moisturizing to keep the skin hydrated, and sun protection to safeguard against harmful UV rays. Proper skincare not only promotes a clear and radiant complexion but also contributes to overall skin health and well-being.

Importance of Skincare:

Skin Health: Skincare routines, when done correctly, can help maintain the skin's natural barrier and balance, protecting it from environmental pollutants and irritants.

Moisture Balance: Moisturizing the skin prevents dryness and helps retain water, ensuring a supple and youthful complexion.

Preventing Premature Aging: Sun protection and anti-aging skincare can reduce the appearance of fine lines, wrinkles, and age spots, promoting youthful-looking skin.

Boosting Self-Confidence: Healthy, clear, and radiant skin can enhance self-confidence and promote a positive self-image.

Preventing Skin Conditions: Regular skincare can help prevent and manage common skin issues such as acne, eczema, and sensitivity.

Skincare Practices:

Cleansing: Cleansing the skin removes dirt, oil, makeup, and impurities accumulated during the day or overnight. It helps unclog pores and prevents breakouts.

Moisturizing: Applying moisturizer nourishes the skin and helps maintain its natural moisture levels. It is essential even for those with oily skin, as it can prevent excessive oil production.

Sun Protection: Using sunscreen with adequate SPF protects the skin from harmful UV rays, preventing sunburn and premature aging and reducing the risk of skin cancer.

Nighttime Skincare: Incorporating a nighttime routine allows the skin to repair and regenerate while one sleeps. This may involve the use of serums, creams, or treatments tailored to specific skin concerns.

Hydration and Nutrition: Staying hydrated and consuming a balanced diet rich in vitamins and antioxidants can promote healthy skin from within.

Illustrations and Examples:

Consider a young man who follows a consistent skincare routine. In the morning, he starts by washing his face with a gentle cleanser, removing any excess oil and impurities. After patting his face dry, he applies a lightweight moisturizer with SPF to protect his skin from the sun's harmful rays throughout the day. In the evening, before going to bed, he cleanses his face again to remove any dirt or pollutants accumulated during the day. He then applies a night cream containing nourishing ingredients to help his skin rejuvenate while he sleeps.

In contrast, imagine another young man who neglects his skincare. He rarely washes his face and does not apply any sunscreen or moisturizer. Over time, his skin becomes prone to breakouts and dryness due to the lack of proper cleansing and hydration. Exposure to the sun without protection may lead to sunburn and an increased risk of premature aging.

Application to a Christian Lifestyle as a Young Man:

Incorporating proper skincare into a Christian lifestyle aligns with principles of stewardship, self-care, and presenting oneself with respect and dignity. Here's how it applies:

Stewardship of the Body: As mentioned earlier, Christians view their bodies as temples of the Holy Spirit. Taking care of the skin through skincare is an act of stewardship, acknowledging that the body is a gift from God.

Self-Care and Respect: Caring for one's skin reflects a level of self-respect and self-care. By investing time and effort in skincare, a young man demonstrates value for his well-being and health.

Presentation and Modesty: Proper skincare can enhance the appearance of the skin without excessive focus on appearance or vanity. It allows a young man to present himself modestly, respecting his own body as well as others.

Responsibility in Decision-Making: Making informed choices about skincare products and practices involves being responsible and mindful of their potential effects on the body and the environment.

Service to Others: Taking care of one's skin can also translate into a more comfortable and pleasant interaction with others. By practicing good skincare, a young man presents himself in a way that is considerate of those around him.

In finally, skincare is an essential aspect of maintaining healthy and radiant skin. As a young man following a Christian lifestyle, incorporating proper skincare aligns with principles of stewardship, self-care, respect, and modesty. By taking care of his skin, he not only enhances his physical appearance but also reflects Christian values through practical acts of caring for himself and presenting himself with humility and responsibility.

Nail Care: Understanding the Importance of Keeping Nails Clean, Trimmed, and Well-Groomed

Nail care is an essential aspect of personal grooming that involves maintaining clean, trimmed, and well-groomed nails. Proper nail care not only enhances the appearance of the hands but also contributes to overall hygiene and self-presentation. It includes practices such as regular nail trimming, cleaning, moisturizing, and protecting nails from damage.

Importance of Nail Care:

Hygiene and Cleanliness: Clean and well-maintained nails are essential for overall hygiene. Regular cleaning removes dirt, bacteria, and potential pathogens that can accumulate under the nails.

Preventing Infections: Trimmed and clean nails reduce the risk of nail infections, which can lead to painful conditions and affect daily activities.

Presentable Appearance: Groomed nails present a neat and polished image, reflecting attention to detail and personal care.

Protecting the Nail Bed: Proper nail care, including appropriate trimming, helps protect the delicate nail bed from damage and injuries.

Avoiding Nail Biting: By maintaining well-groomed nails, individuals are less likely to engage in unhealthy habits like nail-biting.

Nail Care Practices:

Nail Trimming: Regular nail trimming with clean, sharp clippers helps maintain the nails at a manageable length, preventing them from becoming too long and prone to breaking.

Nail Cleaning: Keeping nails clean involves gently scrubbing them with a soft nail brush and mild soap to remove dirt and bacteria.

Moisturizing: Applying moisturizer or cuticle oil to the nails and surrounding skin helps prevent dryness and maintain healthy nail beds.

Protective Measures: Using gloves while doing household chores or working with harsh chemicals can prevent nail damage and maintain their strength.

Avoiding Excessive Use of Nails: Nails should not be used as tools for opening containers or scratching surfaces, as this can lead to damage and weakening of the nails.

Illustrations and Examples:

Consider a young man who practices good nail care. He regularly trims his nails to keep them at a reasonable length, avoiding overgrown nails that can snag or break. After trimming, he cleans his nails with a soft brush and soap to remove any dirt or debris. To maintain healthy nails, he applies cuticle oil to keep the nail bed moisturized and protected. Whenever he engages in household chores or other activities that might stress the nails, he wears protective gloves to avoid damage.

In contrast, imagine another young man who neglects nail care. He rarely trims his nails, leading to overgrown and uneven nails. The lack of cleaning allows dirt and grime to accumulate under his nails, making them appear unkempt and unhygienic. The absence of moisturizing causes his nail beds to become dry and susceptible to cracking.

Application to a Christian Lifestyle as a Young Man:

Incorporating proper nail care into a Christian lifestyle aligns with principles of self-care, respect for oneself and others, and presenting oneself modestly and cleanly. Here's how it applies:

Stewardship of the Body: As mentioned earlier, Christians consider their bodies as temples of the Holy Spirit. Taking care of nails through proper grooming is an act of stewardship, acknowledging that the body is a gift from God.

Modesty and Presentation: Maintaining clean, trimmed nails presents a modest and well-groomed appearance. By practicing good nail care, a young man reflects inner values of modesty and self-respect.

Hygiene and Consideration: Keeping nails clean is not only a matter of personal hygiene but also a consideration for others. It shows respect for oneself and those with whom one interacts.

Resisting Unhealthy Habits: Good nail care can help a young man avoid unhealthy habits like nail biting, which may stem from stress or anxiety. By caring for his nails, he promotes healthier behaviors and self-discipline.

Service to Others: Maintaining well-groomed nails can also be seen as a practical way of showing care for others. When interacting with others, well-kept nails present a positive and presentable image.

In summary, nail care is an essential aspect of personal grooming that contributes to overall hygiene, appearance, and self-respect. As a young man following a Christian lifestyle, incorporating proper nail care aligns with principles of stewardship, modesty, hygiene, and consideration for others. By practicing good nail care, he not only enhances his physical appearance but also reflects Christian values through practical acts of self-care and presenting himself with humility and respect.

Shaving and Facial Hair: Understanding Proper Techniques for Grooming Facial Hair

Shaving and facial hair grooming are essential aspects of personal grooming that involve maintaining a neat and well-groomed appearance. For some young men, this may involve shaving facial hair regularly, while for others, it may involve shaping and grooming their beard or mustache. Proper shaving techniques and facial hair grooming not only enhance one's appearance but also contribute to self-confidence and a polished image.

Importance of Shaving and Facial Hair Grooming:

Personal Presentation: Neatly groomed facial hair presents a polished and well-kept image, reflecting attention to detail and personal care.

Professional and Social Interactions: In many professional settings, a clean-shaven or well-groomed beard is often expected. It can positively impact first impressions and interactions with others.

Hygiene and Cleanliness: Proper grooming of facial hair prevents the accumulation of dirt, food particles, and bacteria, contributing to overall hygiene.

Respect for Cultural and Religious Norms: In some cultures or religious practices, certain facial hair styles may have specific meanings or significance. Proper grooming aligns with respecting these norms.

Self-Expression: For those who choose to keep facial hair, grooming allows for self-expression through different styles and shapes.

Shaving and Facial Hair Grooming Practices:

Shaving Techniques: For those who prefer a clean-shaven look, using a sharp razor and shaving cream or gel can help achieve a smooth and comfortable shave. Shaving in the direction of hair growth and moisturizing the skin afterward can minimize irritation.

Beard Grooming: For those with beards or mustaches, regular trimming and shaping help maintain a well-groomed appearance. Beard oil or balm can be used to keep facial hair soft and moisturized.

Hygiene: Regularly cleaning facial hair with mild soap and water, particularly after meals, helps remove any debris and maintain cleanliness.

Personal Preference: Ultimately, facial hair grooming is a matter of personal preference. Whether a young man chooses to be clean-shaven, have a beard, or sport a mustache, proper grooming is key to presenting a polished and well-maintained appearance.

Illustrations and Examples:

Consider a young man who prefers a clean-shaven look. He starts by moistening his face with warm water, then applies a shaving cream to soften the hair. Using a sharp razor, he shaves in the direction of hair growth, taking care to rinse the razor frequently. After shaving, he rinses his face with cold water to close the pores and applies a soothing aftershave balm to reduce any potential irritation.

On the other hand, imagine a young man who prefers a beard. He regularly trims his beard to maintain a well-groomed length and shape.

He uses a beard comb to keep his facial hair neat and free from tangles. Applying beard oil helps keep his beard soft and adds a subtle shine.

Application to a Christian Lifestyle as a Young Man:

Incorporating proper shaving and facial hair grooming into a Christian lifestyle aligns with principles of self-respect, modesty, and cultural sensitivity. Here's how it applies:

Modesty and Presentation: Proper grooming, whether clean-shaven or with facial hair, allows a young man to present himself modestly and respectfully. A well-groomed appearance reflects inner values of self-respect and humility.

Respect for Others: Facial hair grooming, particularly in cultures or religious settings where specific facial hair styles hold significance, demonstrates respect for others' beliefs and practices.

Professionalism and Service: In professional and social settings, a polished appearance can positively impact interactions and service to others. A young man's well-groomed appearance reflects professionalism and consideration for those around him.

Hygiene and Cleanliness: Regular grooming of facial hair contributes to overall hygiene and cleanliness, showing consideration for oneself and others.

Cultural Awareness: Understanding and respecting cultural norms related to facial hair grooming can promote cultural awareness and inclusivity.

In summary, proper shaving techniques and facial hair grooming are important aspects of personal grooming. As a young man following a Christian lifestyle, incorporating these practices aligns with principles of self-respect, modesty, and cultural sensitivity. By grooming facial hair properly, he not only enhances his appearance but also reflects Christian values through practical acts of consideration, respect, and service to others.

Deodorant and Antiperspirant Use: Understanding the Importance of Managing Body Odor and Sweat

Deodorant and antiperspirant are personal care products designed to manage body odor and sweat, particularly under the arms. These products play a crucial role in maintaining personal hygiene and promoting confidence in social and professional settings. Understanding the difference between deodorants and antiperspirants can help individuals choose the right product based on their specific needs.

Importance of Deodorant and Antiperspirant Use:

Body Odor Management: Sweat itself is odorless, but when it comes into contact with bacteria on the skin's surface, it can produce an unpleasant odor. Deodorants are designed to mask or neutralize body odor, keeping individuals feeling fresh and confident throughout the day.

Sweat Control: Antiperspirants, in addition to addressing body odor, also contain ingredients that temporarily block sweat glands, reducing the amount of sweat produced in the underarm area.

Social Confidence: Properly managing body odor and sweat can boost self-confidence, allowing individuals to feel more at ease in social and professional interactions.

Hygiene and Cleanliness: Using deodorant or antiperspirant is an important aspect of personal hygiene, ensuring that body odor is not a distraction in close-quarter interactions.

Deodorant and Antiperspirant Use Practices:

Application: Deodorants and antiperspirants are typically applied to clean, dry underarms. One should follow the product's instructions for the recommended amount to use.

Choosing the Right Product: Individuals can select deodorants or antiperspirants based on their specific needs and preferences. Some may prefer deodorants for odor control, while others may opt for antiperspirants for additional sweat reduction.

Sensitive Skin Considerations: For those with sensitive skin, it is essential to choose products that are hypoallergenic and free from potential irritants.

Reapplication: Depending on individual activity levels and personal preferences, reapplication of deodorant or antiperspirant throughout the day may be necessary.

Illustrations and Examples:

Imagine a young man preparing for an important job interview on a hot summer day. Before leaving, he applies antiperspirant to his underarms to manage sweat and ensure he feels confident and dry during the interview. The antiperspirant's sweat-blocking properties keep him comfortable and composed, while the deodorant aspect neutralizes any potential body odor, allowing him to focus on the interview without distraction.

On another occasion, consider a young man going to a social event. He chooses a deodorant with a pleasant scent that complements his personal preferences. Throughout the evening, he feels fresh and odor-free, enjoying the event and interacting with others with confidence.

Application to a Christian Lifestyle as a Young Man:

Incorporating proper deodorant and antiperspirant use into a Christian lifestyle aligns with principles of self-respect, modesty, and consideration for others. Here's how it applies:

Modesty and Presentation: Using deodorant or antiperspirant promotes a modest and well-groomed appearance. A young man who takes care of his body odor and sweat reflects inner values of self-respect and humility.

Consideration for Others: Proper hygiene, including managing body odor and sweat, shows consideration for oneself and those with whom one interacts. It allows for more pleasant and comfortable social interactions with others.

Confidence in Service: Feeling confident and at ease in social and professional settings can positively impact interactions and service to others. A young man who uses deodorant or antiperspirant is better equipped to focus on the needs of others.

Hygiene and Cleanliness: Properly managing body odor and sweat contributes to overall hygiene and cleanliness, reflecting responsible stewardship of the body.

Cultural Awareness: Recognizing the importance of personal hygiene and grooming can promote cultural awareness and inclusivity, reflecting Christian values of acceptance and love for all.

In conclusion, using deodorant or antiperspirant is a vital aspect of personal hygiene and grooming. As a young man following a Christian lifestyle, incorporating these practices aligns with principles of self-respect, modesty, and consideration for others. By managing body odor and sweat, he not only enhances his appearance but also reflects Christian values through practical acts of caring for himself and presenting himself with humility and respect for others.

Clothing Care: Understanding the Importance of Laundering and Maintaining Clean and Presentable Clothes

Clothing care is a crucial aspect of personal hygiene and presentation that involves learning how to launder and maintain clothes to keep them clean, fresh, and well-preserved. Proper clothing care not only promotes a polished appearance but also contributes to overall cleanliness and respect for oneself and others. It includes practices such as regular laundering, storing clothes appropriately, and mending minor damages to extend their lifespan.

Importance of Clothing Care:

Hygiene and Cleanliness: Regularly laundering clothes helps remove dirt, sweat, and bacteria accumulated during wear, ensuring cleanliness and personal hygiene.

Presentation and Self-Confidence: Well-maintained and freshly laundered clothes present a polished and well-groomed image, promoting self-confidence and a positive self-image.

Longevity of Clothes: Proper clothing care, such as gentle laundering and appropriate storage, helps preserve the quality and longevity of garments.

Consideration for Others: Maintaining clean and odor-free clothes shows consideration for others in shared spaces, such as workplaces, public transport, or social gatherings.

Clothing Care Practices:

Laundering: Following the care instructions on clothing labels, sorting clothes by color and fabric, and using appropriate washing cycles and detergents are essential for proper laundering.

Stain Removal: Promptly treating stains with suitable stain removers or natural remedies before laundering can help prevent permanent damage to clothes.

Drying: Drying clothes according to fabric guidelines, either by line drying or using a dryer with appropriate settings, prevents shrinkage and preserves the garment's shape.

Ironing and Steaming: Ironing or steaming clothes, when needed, helps maintain a neat and wrinkle-free appearance.

Proper Storage: Storing clothes in a clean and well-ventilated space, using appropriate hangers or folding techniques, helps prevent wrinkles and maintains garment shape.

Illustrations and Examples:

Imagine a young man who follows proper clothing care practices. He sorts his laundry by color and fabric before washing. He uses a gentle cycle and a mild detergent to launder delicate fabrics like wool or silk. After washing, he carefully hangs or folds his clothes to avoid wrinkles. If he notices any stains, he promptly treats them with stain removers before washing the garment. By following these practices, his clothes remain clean, well-preserved, and presentable.

In contrast, consider a scenario where a young man neglects clothing care. He mixes all his clothes together without sorting, leading to color bleeding and fabric damage during washing. He uses a harsh detergent that damages delicate fabrics, causing them to lose their quality over time. Additionally, he often leaves his clothes piled up in a damp environment, resulting in musty odors and mildew growth.

Application to a Christian Lifestyle as a Young Man:

Incorporating proper clothing care into a Christian lifestyle aligns with principles of self-respect, stewardship, and consideration for others. Here's how it applies:

Stewardship of Resources: Proper clothing care, including gentle laundering and mending minor damages, aligns with responsible stewardship of resources. It reflects a conscious effort to preserve the quality and longevity of clothing, reducing waste.

Hygiene and Cleanliness: Clean and well-maintained clothes are essential for personal hygiene and cleanliness. A young man who takes care of his clothing demonstrates self-respect and consideration for others in shared spaces.

Presentation and Modesty: Maintaining clean and wrinkle-free clothes promotes a modest and presentable appearance. By taking care of his clothing, a young man reflects inner values of self-respect and humility.

Respect for God's Creation: Christians believe in honoring God's creation, which includes the resources used to make clothing. Proper clothing care shows appreciation for the materials and labor that go into creating garments.

Consideration for Others: Practicing clothing care contributes to a more pleasant and respectful environment when interacting with others. A young man who maintains clean and odor-free clothes shows consideration for those around him.

In conclusion, clothing care is a crucial aspect of personal hygiene, presentation, and stewardship. As a young man following a Christian lifestyle, incorporating proper clothing care aligns with principles of self-respect, stewardship, and consideration for others. By taking care of his clothes, he not only enhances his appearance but also reflects Christian values through practical acts of caring for himself, preserving resources, and presenting himself with humility and respect for others.

Foot Care: Understanding the Significance of Foot Hygiene and Proper Footwear

Foot care is an essential aspect of personal hygiene and overall well-being, focusing on the health and cleanliness of the feet. Proper foot care involves regular washing, wearing suitable footwear, and addressing foot-related issues to prevent discomfort and maintain foot health. Taking care of the feet not only promotes physical comfort but also reflects consideration for oneself and others in daily interactions.

Importance of Foot Care:

Personal Hygiene: Regularly washing and caring for the feet helps prevent the buildup of dirt, sweat, and bacteria, contributing to overall personal hygiene.

Foot Health: Proper foot care minimizes the risk of foot-related issues such as athlete's foot, fungal infections, or foot odor.

Physical Comfort: Maintaining healthy feet ensures physical comfort, allowing individuals to move and stand without pain or discomfort.

Preventing Foot Pain: Addressing foot-related issues promptly, such as blisters or ingrown toenails, can prevent unnecessary foot pain and discomfort.

Foot Care Practices:

Daily Washing: Washing the feet daily with warm water and mild soap helps remove dirt and sweat, reducing the risk of fungal infections and foot odor.

Drying and Moisturizing: After washing, thoroughly drying the feet, especially between the toes, helps prevent moisture buildup. Applying moisturizer to the feet keeps the skin hydrated.

Proper Footwear: Wearing well-fitting and supportive footwear suitable for various activities helps maintain proper foot alignment and prevents foot strain.

Foot Protection: Using appropriate foot protection, such as socks or shoes in public places, helps prevent infections and injuries.

Addressing Foot Issues: Promptly addressing foot-related issues, such as blisters, calluses, or ingrown toenails, can prevent them from worsening and causing discomfort.

Illustrations and Examples:

Imagine a young man who practices good foot care. Every morning and evening, he washes his feet with warm water and mild soap, ensuring they are thoroughly clean. After drying his feet, he applies a moisturizing foot cream to keep the skin soft and hydrated. When selecting footwear, he chooses shoes that fit well and provide adequate support, ensuring his feet are comfortable throughout the day. He also wears socks to protect his feet and prevent friction, reducing the risk of blisters and calluses.

In contrast, consider a scenario where a young man neglects foot care. He rarely washes his feet and wears the same shoes without proper support or cushioning for extended periods. Over time, his feet develop calluses and blisters due to friction and pressure, causing discomfort and pain.

Application to a Christian Lifestyle as a Young Man:

Incorporating proper foot care into a Christian lifestyle aligns with principles of self-care, respect for oneself and others, and stewardship of the body. Here's how it applies:

Stewardship of the Body: Proper foot care reflects responsible stewardship of the body, recognizing that the feet are a precious part of God's creation that deserves care and attention.

Humility and Modesty: Taking care of the feet demonstrates humility and modesty, recognizing that every part of the body deserves care and respect.

Consideration for Others: Practicing foot hygiene, such as washing the feet regularly and wearing clean socks, shows consideration for others in shared spaces, such as households, workplaces, or public places.

Service and Compassion: By maintaining healthy feet, a young man can better engage in acts of service and compassion, knowing that physical comfort allows him to focus on the needs of others.

Physical and Spiritual Well-Being: Addressing foot-related issues promptly contributes to physical well-being and can positively impact one's overall mood and spiritual well-being.

In conclusion, foot care is an important aspect of personal hygiene and well-being. As a young man following a Christian lifestyle, incorporating proper foot care aligns with principles of stewardship, humility, consideration for others, and self-respect. By taking care of his feet, he not only enhances his physical well-being but also reflects Christian values through practical acts of caring for himself and presenting himself with humility and respect for others.

Personal Odor Management: Understanding the Importance of Managing Body Odors

Personal odor management is a critical aspect of personal hygiene and self-presentation that involves being aware of body odors and taking appropriate measures to manage them effectively. Body odors can arise from various factors, including sweat, bacteria on the skin, or certain foods consumed. Managing personal odors not only promotes cleanliness and comfort but also reflects consideration for oneself and others in social and professional interactions.

Importance of Personal Odor Management:

Personal Hygiene: Addressing body odors through proper hygiene, such as regular bathing and using deodorants, contributes to overall personal cleanliness.

Self-Confidence: Managing body odors can boost self-confidence, allowing individuals to feel comfortable and at ease in social and professional settings.

Consideration for Others: Being mindful of personal odors shows consideration for others in shared spaces, such as public transportation, workplaces, or social gatherings.

Respect for God's Creation: Christians believe in honoring God's creation, which includes the human body. Proper personal odor management reflects a responsible stewardship of the body.

Personal Odor Management Practices:

Regular Bathing/Showering: Daily bathing or showering helps remove sweat and bacteria from the skin, reducing the likelihood of body odor.

Proper Clothing Care: Laundering clothes regularly and wearing clean clothes each day helps prevent odor buildup.

Deodorant and Antiperspirant Use: Using deodorants or antiperspirants helps mask or neutralize body odor and manage sweat effectively.

Foot Hygiene: Proper foot care, including washing, drying, and wearing clean socks and shoes, helps manage foot-related odors.

Awareness of Diet: Being mindful of the foods consumed, especially those with strong odors, can influence personal body odor.

Illustrations and Examples:

Imagine a young man who practices good personal odor management. He starts his day with a refreshing shower, thoroughly washing his body and hair. After drying off, he applies deodorant to his underarms to manage sweat and body odor throughout the day. He puts on clean and well-maintained clothes, ensuring they are free from odors and stains. Throughout the day, he remains mindful of his hygiene and avoids consuming foods that might cause strong body odors.

On the other hand, consider a scenario where a young man neglects personal odor management. He frequently skips bathing, leading to a buildup of sweat and bacteria on his skin. He rarely uses deodorant or antiperspirant, causing body odor to become noticeable. Additionally, he wears unwashed or soiled clothes, exacerbating the issue.

Application to a Christian Lifestyle as a Young Man:

Incorporating proper personal odor management into a Christian lifestyle aligns with principles of self-care, respect for oneself and others, and stewardship of the body. Here's how it applies:

Stewardship of the Body: Proper personal odor management reflects responsible stewardship of the body, acknowledging it as a gift from God that deserves care and attention.

Modesty and Consideration for Others: Being mindful of personal odors demonstrates modesty and consideration for others. A young man who takes care of his hygiene is better equipped to interact with others in a considerate manner.

Respect for God's Creation: Christians view the human body as a sacred creation of God. Proper personal odor management reflects a sense of reverence and respect for this divine gift.

Service and Outreach: By managing personal odors, a young man can engage in acts of service and outreach with confidence, knowing that his personal hygiene allows him to focus on the needs of others.

Cultural Sensitivity: Being aware of personal odors is also essential in diverse cultural settings where certain odors might be perceived differently.

In conclusion, personal odor management is a fundamental aspect of personal hygiene and self-presentation. As a young man following a Christian lifestyle, incorporating proper odor management aligns with principles of stewardship, respect for oneself and others, and consideration in social interactions. By managing personal odors effectively, he not only promotes cleanliness and comfort but also reflects Christian values through practical acts of caring for himself and presenting himself with humility and respect for others.

Menstrual Hygiene (for Females): Understanding the Importance of Menstrual Hygiene Practices

Menstrual hygiene is a vital aspect of women's health that involves learning about proper practices during menstruation to ensure cleanliness, comfort, and overall well-being. It encompasses using and disposing of menstrual products correctly and maintaining good personal hygiene during this natural bodily process. While menstruation is a topic specific to females, it is essential for young men in a Christian lifestyle to be knowledgeable and understanding to support their female friends, family members, and colleagues.

Importance of Menstrual Hygiene:

Health and Comfort: Proper menstrual hygiene practices contribute to women's physical health and comfort during menstruation, reducing the risk of infections and discomfort.

Confidence and Dignity: Maintaining good menstrual hygiene allows women to feel confident and maintain their dignity during menstruation, enabling them to participate in daily activities without hindrance.

Social Inclusion: Ensuring menstrual hygiene enables women to participate fully in social and professional life, promoting gender equity and inclusion.

Cultural Sensitivity: Being informed about menstrual hygiene practices allows young men to be culturally sensitive and understanding in diverse settings.

Menstrual Hygiene Practices:

Using Menstrual Products: Women have various options for menstrual products, such as sanitary pads, tampons, menstrual cups, or reusable cloth pads. Understanding how to use these products safely and effectively is essential.

Regular Changing: Menstrual products should be changed regularly to prevent odor, discomfort, and the risk of infection. The frequency of changing depends on the product type and individual flow.

Washing and Cleaning: Maintaining good personal hygiene, including washing hands before and after handling menstrual products, is crucial.

Disposal of Products: Menstrual products should be disposed of properly to prevent environmental pollution and promote sanitation.

Illustrations and Examples:

Consider a young woman who practices proper menstrual hygiene. During her period, she uses sanitary pads and changes them every 4-6 hours to stay fresh and comfortable. Before and after handling menstrual products, she washes her hands with soap and water. When disposing of used pads, she wraps them in paper and disposes of them in a waste bin with a lid to maintain privacy and prevent odors.

On the other hand, imagine a scenario where a young woman neglects menstrual hygiene. She wears the same pad for an extended period, causing discomfort and increasing the risk of infections. She may not wash her hands before handling menstrual products, increasing the chances of bacterial contamination.

Application to a Christian Lifestyle as a Young Man:

While menstruation is a topic specific to females, young men in a Christian lifestyle can apply certain principles to support women around them and promote understanding and respect. Here's how it applies:

Empathy and Understanding: Demonstrating empathy and understanding towards menstruation fosters a compassionate and supportive environment for the women in their lives.

Respecting Privacy and Dignity: Men can respect the privacy and dignity of women during menstruation by providing a safe and supportive environment.

Cultural Sensitivity: Being informed about menstrual hygiene practices and customs in different cultures promotes cultural sensitivity and inclusivity.

Support and Advocacy: Young men can advocate for access to menstrual hygiene products and education to support women's health and well-being.

In conclusion, menstrual hygiene is a crucial aspect of women's health and well-being. While it is specific to females, young men in a Christian lifestyle can apply principles of empathy, respect, and cultural sensitivity to support the women in their lives during menstruation. By promoting understanding and providing a supportive environment, they contribute to a more compassionate and inclusive community.

Pubic Hair Grooming (if Desired): Understanding Grooming Options and Techniques for Personal Comfort

Pubic hair grooming is a personal choice that some individuals may consider for reasons related to personal comfort, aesthetics, or cultural preferences. Grooming options can range from complete removal to trimming or shaping the pubic hair. While this topic is specific to individuals who may have pubic hair, it is essential for young men in a Christian lifestyle to approach it with sensitivity and understanding.

Understanding Grooming Options:

Complete Removal (Shaving/Waxing): Some individuals may choose to remove all pubic hair through methods such as shaving or waxing. This option provides a smooth and hair-free appearance.

Trimming: Trimming the pubic hair involves cutting the hair to a shorter length for a neater look while still maintaining some hair coverage.

Shaping: Shaping involves creating specific patterns or designs with the pubic hair using trimming techniques.

Natural Growth: Some individuals may choose not to groom their pubic hair at all and let it grow naturally.

Importance of Sensitivity and Personal Choice:

Respecting Personal Autonomy: Pubic hair grooming is a personal choice, and individuals should be free to make decisions based on their own comfort and preferences.

Avoiding Pressure or Judgment: Young men should avoid pressuring others or passing judgment based on their grooming choices. Respect and understanding are vital in supporting each individual's autonomy.

Application to a Christian Lifestyle as a Young Man:

As a young man in a Christian lifestyle, it is essential to approach discussions about pubic hair grooming with sensitivity and understanding. Here's how it applies:

Respect for Personal Choices: Respecting the personal choices of others, regardless of grooming preferences, reflects Christian values of love, acceptance, and non-judgment.

Modesty and Humility: If an individual chooses to groom their pubic hair for modesty or personal comfort, it aligns with principles of modesty and humility.

Cultural Sensitivity: Being sensitive to cultural differences in grooming practices promotes inclusivity and understanding within a diverse community.

Supportive Environment: Creating a supportive environment where individuals feel comfortable discussing personal grooming choices fosters open communication and healthy relationships.

In conclusion, pubic hair grooming is a personal choice that individuals may consider for various reasons. As a young man in a Christian lifestyle, it is crucial to approach this topic with sensitivity and understanding, respecting each person's autonomy and choices. By promoting an environment of acceptance and support, young men can uphold

Christian values of love and respect for others, regardless of their grooming preferences.

Skincare for Specific Concerns: Understanding Skincare for Acne, Dry Skin, or Other Conditions

Skincare for specific skin concerns involves learning about targeted skincare practices and products to address particular issues such as acne, dry skin, or other skin conditions. Each skin concern requires unique approaches and solutions to maintain healthy and vibrant skin. As a young man in a Christian lifestyle, understanding and practicing skincare for specific concerns aligns with principles of self-care, stewardship, and consideration for oneself and others.

Understanding Skincare for Specific Concerns:

Acne-Prone Skin: Acne is a common skin concern characterized by pimples, blackheads, or whiteheads. Skincare for acne-prone skin focuses on controlling excess oil, preventing clogged pores, and reducing inflammation.

Dry Skin: Dry skin lacks moisture and can feel tight or rough. Skincare for dry skin aims to restore and retain moisture, improving the skin's texture and appearance.

Sensitive Skin: Sensitive skin is easily irritated and may react to certain ingredients or environmental factors. Skincare for sensitive skin involves using gentle and hypoallergenic products.

Eczema or Dermatitis: These conditions cause red, itchy, and inflamed patches on the skin. Skincare for eczema or dermatitis focuses on moisturizing and avoiding triggers that exacerbate symptoms.

Skincare Practices for Specific Concerns:

Cleansing: Choosing the right cleanser for the specific skin concern is essential. For acne-prone skin, a gentle, non-comedogenic cleanser helps unclog pores. Dry skin benefits from a hydrating and creamy cleanser.

Moisturizing: Applying a suitable moisturizer helps replenish and lock in moisture for dry skin, while those with acne-prone skin should opt for oil-free, lightweight moisturizers.

Exfoliation: Gentle exfoliation can aid in removing dead skin cells and promoting skin renewal. For acne-prone skin, chemical exfoliants with ingredients like salicylic acid can be beneficial.

Spot Treatments: Targeted spot treatments, such as benzoyl peroxide for acne or hydrocortisone for eczema, can help alleviate specific skin concerns.

Sun Protection: Using sunscreen with adequate SPF protects the skin from harmful UV rays, preventing further damage and irritation.

Illustrations and Examples:

Consider a young man with acne-prone skin. His skincare routine includes cleansing his face twice daily with a gentle, acne-fighting cleanser. He applies an oil-free, non-comedogenic moisturizer to keep his skin hydrated without clogging pores. Once a week, he uses a salicylic acid-based exfoliant to help unclog his pores and prevent breakouts. For spot treatment, he applies a benzoyl peroxide gel to reduce inflammation and redness on active acne spots.

On the other hand, imagine a young man with dry skin. His skincare routine involves using a creamy and hydrating cleanser to prevent further dryness. He follows up with a rich moisturizer containing ingredients like hyaluronic acid to retain moisture. To exfoliate, he uses a gentle scrub once a week to remove dead skin cells without causing irritation.

Application to a Christian Lifestyle as a Young Man:

Incorporating specific skincare practices into a Christian lifestyle aligns with principles of self-care, stewardship, and consideration for oneself and others. Here's how it applies:

Stewardship of the Body: Proper skincare practices demonstrate responsible stewardship of the body, recognizing that the skin is a vital part of God's creation.

Self-Care and Respect: Taking care of the skin reflects self-respect and consideration for one's well-being, promoting a positive self-image.

Empathy and Compassion: Being aware of and supporting others with specific skin concerns fosters empathy and compassion within the community.

Modesty and Humility: Practicing skincare for specific concerns can be a modest and humble act, recognizing the body's vulnerabilities and needs.

Caring for Others: By taking care of their own skin and understanding the challenges of others, young men can better support and care for those around them.

In conclusion, skincare for specific concerns requires tailored approaches to address individual skin needs. As a young man following a Christian lifestyle, understanding and practicing these skincare practices align with principles of self-care, stewardship, empathy, and consideration. By maintaining healthy skin, young men can promote self-respect, respect for others, and a compassionate community that embraces diversity and individual needs.

Sun Protection: Understanding the Importance of Sunscreen and Protective Clothing

Sun protection is a vital aspect of skincare and overall health, involving the use of sunscreen and protective clothing to shield the skin from harmful ultraviolet (UV) rays. Overexposure to the sun's UV rays can lead to sunburn, premature aging, and an increased risk of skin cancer. As a young man in a Christian lifestyle, understanding the significance of sun protection aligns with principles of stewardship, self-care, and showing love and consideration for oneself and others.

Importance of Sun Protection:

Preventing Sunburn: Sunscreen and protective clothing create a barrier that helps prevent sunburn, a painful condition caused by excessive UV exposure.

Reducing Skin Cancer Risk: Prolonged sun exposure is a major risk factor for skin cancer, including melanoma, one of the deadliest forms of cancer. Sun protection reduces this risk significantly.

Preventing Premature Aging: UV rays can damage the skin's collagen fibers, leading to premature wrinkles, sagging, and age spots. Sun protection helps maintain youthful-looking skin.

Maintaining Overall Health: Proper sun protection supports overall health and well-being by reducing the risk of skin damage and potential health complications.

Sun Protection Practices:

Sunscreen Application: Use a broad-spectrum sunscreen with an SPF of at least 30 and apply it generously to all exposed skin areas, including the face, neck, arms, and legs. Reapply every two hours or after swimming or sweating.

Seeking Shade: When the sun is at its peak (usually between 10 a.m. and 4 p.m.), seek shade or stay indoors to minimize UV exposure.

Wearing Protective Clothing: Wear clothing that covers the arms and legs, as well as a wide-brimmed hat and sunglasses to protect the face and eyes.

Avoiding Tanning Beds: Tanning beds also emit harmful UV rays and should be avoided.

Illustrations and Examples:

Imagine a young man going to the beach on a sunny day. Before heading out, he applies a broad-spectrum sunscreen with an SPF of 50 to all exposed areas, ensuring thorough coverage. He wears a long-sleeved rash guard to protect his arms and a wide-brimmed hat to shield his face from direct sun exposure. He also wears sunglasses to protect his eyes from UV rays.

On the contrary, consider a young man who spends long hours outside without sunscreen or protective clothing. After spending the day in the sun, he develops a painful sunburn on his shoulders and neck, which could have been prevented with proper sun protection.

Application to a Christian Lifestyle as a Young Man:

Incorporating sun protection practices into a Christian lifestyle aligns with principles of stewardship, self-care, and love for oneself and others. Here's how it applies:

Stewardship of the Body: Proper sun protection demonstrates responsible stewardship of the body, recognizing that it is a precious gift from God.

Caring for God's Creation: By protecting their skin from harmful UV rays, young men show appreciation for God's creation, including the human body.

Self-Care and Well-Being: Prioritizing sun protection is an act of self-care, promoting physical well-being and healthy skin.

Showing Love and Consideration: By practicing sun protection, young men show love and consideration for their own health and the well-being of others, encouraging a culture of care within the community.

In conclusion, sun protection is a crucial part of maintaining healthy skin and preventing sunburn and skin cancer. As a young man following a Christian lifestyle, understanding the significance of sun protection aligns with principles of stewardship, self-care, and consideration for oneself and others. By practicing sun protection, young men can protect their skin from harmful UV rays and show love and appreciation for the gift of their bodies. They also serve as role models, encouraging others to adopt sun-safe practices for a healthier and happier community.

Proper Handshakes and Basic Etiquette: Understanding Social Grooming for Positive Interactions

Proper handshakes and basic etiquette are essential aspects of social grooming that contribute to positive and respectful interactions in various social situations. These practices involve offering a firm and confident handshake, maintaining eye contact, and adhering to basic etiquette rules to show respect and consideration for others. As a young man in a Christian lifestyle, understanding and practicing proper handshakes and basic etiquette align with principles of kindness, humility, and treating others with love and respect.

Importance of Proper Handshakes and Basic Etiquette:

First Impressions: Proper handshakes and good etiquette create positive first impressions, which are crucial for establishing rapport and respect in social and professional settings.

Showing Respect: Offering a proper handshake and adhering to basic etiquette demonstrates respect for others, their personal space, and cultural norms.

Effective Communication: Maintaining eye contact during conversations fosters effective communication and shows genuine interest in what others have to say.

Building Relationships: Social grooming practices help build strong and meaningful relationships with others, fostering a sense of trust and camaraderie.

Proper Handshake and Basic Etiquette Practices:

Handshakes: Offer a firm handshake that is neither too weak nor too overpowering. Make sure to make palm-to-palm contact and maintain a neutral grip duration. Avoid shaking hands for too long or too briefly.

Eye Contact: During conversations, maintain eye contact without staring intensely, as this can be uncomfortable. It conveys interest and attentiveness in the interaction.

Listening Attentively: When someone is speaking, actively listen without interrupting and show genuine interest in their thoughts and feelings.

Politeness and Gratitude: Use polite language, such as "please" and "thank you," to show appreciation and gratitude in social exchanges.

Respecting Personal Space: Be mindful of personal space boundaries and avoid standing too close to others, especially in unfamiliar or formal settings.

Illustrations and Examples:

Imagine a young man attending a networking event. As he meets new people, he offers a firm and confident handshake, maintaining eye contact and exchanging warm greetings. During conversations, he listens attentively, nodding to show understanding and interest in what others are saying. He uses polite language, saying "please" when making a request and expressing gratitude with a sincere "thank you" when receiving assistance.

On the contrary, consider a young man who attends the same event but neglects proper handshakes and basic etiquette. He offers limp handshakes, avoids eye contact, and appears disinterested during conversations, which can lead to a negative impression on others.

Application to a Christian Lifestyle as a Young Man:

Incorporating proper handshakes and basic etiquette into a Christian lifestyle aligns with principles of kindness, humility, and treating others with love and respect. Here's how it applies:

Treating Others with Respect: Proper handshakes and etiquette show respect for others, reflecting the Christian value of treating all individuals as children of God.

Humility and Servanthood: Displaying good manners and practicing social grooming humbly puts others' needs and feelings before one's own.

Compassion and Empathy: Being attentive and polite in social interactions fosters a sense of compassion and empathy towards others.

Building Christlike Relationships: By adhering to proper handshakes and etiquette, young men can build Christlike relationships based on mutual respect and love.

Being a Positive Influence: Practicing proper handshakes and basic etiquette sets a positive example for others, promoting a culture of kindness and consideration in the community.

In conclusion, proper handshakes and basic etiquette are crucial for fostering positive and respectful interactions in various social situations. As a young man in a Christian lifestyle, understanding and practicing social grooming align with principles of kindness, humility, and treating others with love and respect. By showing consideration and respect in social exchanges, young men can promote a culture of compassion and understanding, reflecting Christ's teachings of love and humility in their interactions with others.

Proper Use of Personal Care Products: Understanding Appropriate and Safe Usage

Understanding how to use personal care products, such as soaps, lotions, and shampoos, appropriately and safely is essential for maintaining healthy skin, hair, and overall well-being. Proper use ensures that the products provide their intended benefits without causing harm or adverse effects. As a young man in a Christian lifestyle, practicing proper use of personal care products aligns with principles of stewardship, self-care, and consideration for one's body as a temple of the Holy Spirit.

Importance of Proper Use of Personal Care Products:

Effective Results: Using personal care products appropriately ensures that they deliver their intended benefits, such as cleansing, moisturizing, or nourishing the skin and hair.

Safety and Avoiding Adverse Effects: Proper usage minimizes the risk of allergic reactions, skin irritations, or other adverse effects caused by misuse or overuse of products.

Economical Use: Understanding how much product to use and how often ensures that the products last longer, leading to cost-effectiveness.

Sustainable Practices: Proper use of personal care products aligns with sustainable practices, reducing waste and environmental impact.

Proper Use of Personal Care Products:

Soaps and Body Washes: Apply an appropriate amount of soap or body wash onto wet hands or a bath sponge, lather it, and then gently massage onto the skin. Rinse thoroughly with water afterward.

Shampoos and Conditioners: Apply a small amount of shampoo to wet hair, lather it, and gently massage the scalp. Rinse thoroughly and follow with a conditioner, applying it to the ends of the hair and avoiding the scalp.

Moisturizers and Lotions: Apply an adequate amount of moisturizer or lotion onto clean, dry skin. Gently massage it in until fully absorbed.

Sunscreen: Apply a generous amount of sunscreen with at least SPF 30 to all exposed areas of the skin before going outdoors. Reapply every two hours or after swimming or sweating.

Illustrations and Examples:

Imagine a young man starting his morning routine. He uses an appropriate amount of body wash in the shower, lathering it up before gently massaging it onto his skin. After rinsing, he applies a small amount of shampoo to his wet hair, ensuring it covers his scalp and hair evenly. He rinses thoroughly and then applies conditioner to the ends of his hair before washing it off.

Later in the day, he applies sunscreen with an SPF of 50 to all exposed areas of his skin before heading outside for an outdoor activity. He makes sure to reapply every two hours to maintain protection from the sun.

On the contrary, consider a young man who uses excessive amounts of soap and shampoo during his shower. He forgets to rinse off all the shampoo from his hair, leading to product buildup and discomfort.

Application to a Christian Lifestyle as a Young Man:

Practicing proper use of personal care products aligns with principles of stewardship, self-care, and treating the body as a temple of the Holy Spirit in a Christian lifestyle. Here's how it applies:

Stewardship of the Body: Using personal care products appropriately reflects responsible stewardship of the body, recognizing it as a gift from God that deserves proper care.

Self-Care and Respect: Properly caring for the body through personal care practices demonstrates self-respect and respect for the body as God's creation.

Caring for God's Temple: Treating the body with care aligns with the Christian belief of considering the body as a temple of the Holy Spirit (1 Corinthians 6:19-20).

Gratitude for God's Gifts: Practicing proper use of personal care products reflects gratitude for the gifts of health and well-being that God has bestowed upon us.

Consideration for Others: Being mindful of using appropriate amounts of products also demonstrates consideration for others, as it promotes sustainable practices and reduces waste.

In conclusion, understanding the proper use of personal care products is crucial for effective results, safety, and sustainable practices. As a young man following a Christian lifestyle, practicing proper use aligns with principles of stewardship, self-care, and consideration for one's body as a temple of the Holy Spirit. By using personal care products responsibly, young men can maintain healthy skin, hair, and overall well-being while showing gratitude and respect for the body, a precious gift from God.

Caring for Personal Items: Ensuring Hygiene and Responsible Stewardship

Caring for personal items, such as toothbrushes, hairbrushes, and razors, is essential for maintaining proper hygiene and prolonging the life of these items. Proper care involves regular cleaning, storing items appropriately, and replacing them when necessary. As a young man in a Christian lifestyle, understanding and practicing care for personal items align with principles of responsible stewardship, self-care, and consideration for oneself and others.

Importance of Caring for Personal Items:

Hygiene and Health: Properly caring for personal items helps prevent the buildup of bacteria, reducing the risk of infections and maintaining good hygiene.

Cost-Effectiveness: Regular maintenance and cleaning of personal items contribute to their longevity, saving money in the long run by avoiding premature replacements.

Respect for Belongings: Caring for personal items demonstrates respect for one's possessions, recognizing them as valuable resources.

Consideration for Others: Proper hygiene practices and maintaining clean personal items show consideration for others when sharing spaces.

Caring for Personal Items Practices:

Toothbrushes: Rinse toothbrushes thoroughly with water after each use to remove toothpaste and debris. Store them in an upright position to allow them to air dry. Replace toothbrushes every three to four months or sooner if the bristles become frayed.

Hairbrushes: Remove hair from hairbrushes regularly and wash them with mild soap and water every one to two weeks. Allow them to air dry completely before using them again.

Razors: Rinse razors thoroughly after each use to remove hair and shaving cream. Store them in a dry area to prevent moisture buildup and rust. Replace razors regularly, especially if they become dull or rusty.

Other Personal Items: Clean other personal items, such as combs, nail clippers, and tweezers, regularly using soap and water. Disinfect them with rubbing alcohol to further prevent bacterial growth.

Illustrations and Examples:

Consider a young man who diligently cares for his personal items. After brushing his teeth in the morning, he rinses his toothbrush thoroughly under running water and places it in a holder to dry. He makes a mental note to replace his toothbrush in three months. Later, after shaving, he rinses his razor carefully and dries it before storing it in a dry cabinet. He replaces the razor blade regularly to ensure an effective and safe shave.

On the other hand, imagine a young man who neglects to care for his personal items. He leaves his toothbrush lying flat on the bathroom counter without rinsing it properly. As a result, bacteria accumulate on the toothbrush bristles, increasing the risk of oral health issues.

Application to a Christian Lifestyle as a Young Man:

Caring for personal items aligns with principles of responsible stewardship, self-care, and consideration for oneself and others in a Christian lifestyle. Here's how it applies:

Stewardship of Possessions: Properly caring for personal items demonstrates responsible stewardship of the possessions God has provided.

Respect for the Body as God's Temple: By maintaining personal items and ensuring proper hygiene, young men show respect for their bodies as temples of the Holy Spirit (1 Corinthians 6:19-20).

Self-Care and Personal Responsibility: Caring for personal items reflects a sense of personal responsibility and self-care, which are essential aspects of a healthy and balanced Christian life.

Consideration for Others: Proper hygiene practices and maintenance of personal items show consideration for others when sharing spaces or personal belongings.

Humility and Gratitude: By caring for personal items, young men practice humility and gratitude for the resources they have been blessed with.

In conclusion, caring for personal items is crucial for maintaining hygiene, prolonging one's life, and showing respect for one's possessions. As a young man in a Christian lifestyle, understanding and practicing proper care aligns with principles of responsible stewardship, self-care, and consideration for oneself and others. By treating personal items with care, young men can demonstrate responsible ownership and create a hygienic and respectful environment for themselves and those around them.

Understanding Body Changes: Adapting Hygiene Routines During Puberty

Understanding the physical changes that occur during puberty is crucial for young men to navigate this transformative phase in their lives. As the body goes through various changes, it's essential to adapt hygiene routines accordingly to promote good health, self-confidence, and self-care. As a young man in a Christian lifestyle, gaining knowledge about body changes aligns with principles of stewardship, self-acceptance, and understanding the gift of the human body created by God.

Importance of Understanding Body Changes:

Self-Awareness: Understanding body changes during puberty helps young men become more self-aware and comfortable with their developing bodies.

Hygiene and Health: Adapting hygiene routines according to changing needs ensures good physical health and prevents hygiene-related issues.

Self-Confidence: Having knowledge about body changes promotes self-confidence, empowering young men to embrace their bodies with acceptance and appreciation.

Responsible Stewardship: Understanding the body's development and its needs reflects responsible stewardship of the gift of the human body.

Understanding Body Changes During Puberty:

Growth Spurts: Young men experience rapid growth spurts during puberty, which can result in height and muscle changes.

Hormonal Changes: Hormones fluctuate during puberty, leading to physical changes such as the growth of facial hair, body hair, and deepening of the voice.

Skin Changes: Increased oil production during puberty can lead to acne breakouts and oily skin.

Sweat and Body Odor: Hormonal changes also lead to increased sweat production and body odor.

Adapting Hygiene Routines:

Personal Hygiene: Emphasize daily showering or bathing to cleanse the skin and remove excess sweat and oils. Use a gentle cleanser to prevent skin irritation.

Facial Care: Develop a skincare routine to address acne and oily skin. Use products with ingredients like salicylic acid to help control breakouts.

Oral Hygiene: Maintain good oral hygiene by brushing teeth at least twice a day, flossing, and visiting the dentist regularly.

Hair Care: Adjust hair care routines based on hair type and changes during puberty. Use shampoos and conditioners that address specific hair needs.

Deodorant Use: Start using deodorant or antiperspirant to manage sweat and body odor effectively.

Illustrations and Examples:

Consider a young man going through puberty. He notices changes in his skin, including acne breakouts and oiliness. He adapts his skincare routine, using a gentle cleanser to wash his face twice a day and applying a salicylic acid-based spot treatment for acne. He also starts using deodorant daily to manage body odor effectively.

On the other hand, imagine a young man experiencing body odor and sweating more frequently but neglecting to use deodorant or adjust his hygiene routine. As a result, he may become self-conscious about body odor, affecting his confidence and social interactions.

Application to a Christian Lifestyle as a Young Man:

Understanding body changes and adapting hygiene routines aligns with principles of responsible stewardship, self-acceptance, and recognizing the gift of the human body in a Christian lifestyle. Here's how it applies:

Stewardship of the Body: Gaining knowledge about body changes reflects responsible stewardship of the body, acknowledging it as a gift from God to be cared for and respected.

Self-Acceptance and Confidence: Understanding body changes promotes self-acceptance, encouraging young men to embrace their bodies with confidence and appreciation for God's creation.

Respect and Modesty: Practicing good hygiene and adapting routines reflects respect for oneself and others, aligning with Christian values of modesty and humility.

Supportive Environment: Creating a supportive environment where young men can openly discuss body changes fosters empathy, compassion, and a sense of community.

Prayer and Gratitude: In times of change and adaptation, young men can turn to prayer and express gratitude for the gift of their bodies and the journey of growth.

In conclusion, understanding body changes during puberty and adapting hygiene routines accordingly is crucial for young men's self-awareness, confidence, and physical well-being. As a young man in a

Christian lifestyle, gaining knowledge about body changes aligns with principles of stewardship, self-acceptance, and acknowledging the gift of the human body created by God. By adopting hygiene routines and practicing good self-care, young men can navigate puberty with confidence and respect for themselves and others, fostering a positive and supportive community.

Overall, Body Wellness: The Holistic Importance of Personal Hygiene

Understanding that personal hygiene goes beyond appearance and is integral to maintaining overall health and wellness is crucial for young men. Proper hygiene practices not only contribute to a clean and well-groomed appearance but also have a significant impact on physical and mental well-being. As a young man in a Christian lifestyle, valuing overall body wellness through personal hygiene aligns with principles of stewardship, self-care, and recognizing the body as a temple of the Holy Spirit.

Importance of Overall Body Wellness through Personal Hygiene:

Physical Health: Good personal hygiene practices, such as regular bathing, dental care, and handwashing, help prevent the spread of diseases and infections.

Mental Well-Being: Proper personal hygiene promotes a positive self-image and boosts self-confidence, contributing to better mental health.

Social Interactions: Maintaining personal hygiene enhances social interactions, as others are more likely to feel comfortable and at ease around a person who takes care of their appearance and cleanliness.

Spiritual Connection: Recognizing the body as a temple of the Holy Spirit (1 Corinthians 6:19-20), young men understand the importance of caring for their bodies as a way of honoring God's gift.

Understanding the Holistic Impact of Personal Hygiene:

Physical Hygiene: Regular bathing, washing hands, and maintaining oral hygiene are essential for removing germs, preventing infections, and promoting overall physical health.

Skin Care: Proper skincare, including cleansing and moisturizing, helps maintain skin health, prevent dryness, and reduce the risk of skin conditions.

Oral Health: Dental care practices like brushing, flossing, and regular dental check-ups are vital for maintaining strong teeth, healthy gums, and overall oral hygiene.

Hair Care: Good hair care practices, such as regular washing, conditioning, and trimming, contribute to healthy hair and scalp.

Nail Care: Keeping nails clean and well-groomed prevents the accumulation of dirt and bacteria, promoting overall hand hygiene.

Proper Nutrition: A balanced and nutritious diet contributes to overall body wellness, promoting healthy skin, hair, and nails.

Physical Activity: Engaging in regular physical activity not only benefits physical health but also contributes to mental well-being.

Mental and Emotional Well-Being: Practicing good personal hygiene fosters a positive self-image, boosting self-confidence and mental well-being.

Illustrations and Examples:

Imagine a young man who prioritizes overall body wellness through personal hygiene. He starts his day by taking a refreshing shower and thoroughly cleaning his body. After that, he brushes his teeth, flosses, and uses mouthwash to maintain oral hygiene. He follows a skincare routine, cleansing and moisturizing his face to keep his skin healthy.

Later in the day, he engages in physical activity like jogging or playing sports, contributing to his overall physical and mental well-being. He ensures his nails are clean and neatly trimmed and regularly washes his hands to prevent the spread of germs.

On the other hand, consider a young man who neglects personal hygiene. He rarely showers, neglects oral care, and seldom washes his hands. As a result, he may experience frequent illnesses due to compromised immunity and suffer from poor self-confidence and social discomfort.

Application to a Christian Lifestyle as a Young Man:

Valuing overall body wellness through personal hygiene aligns with principles of stewardship, self-care, and recognizing the body as a temple of the Holy Spirit. Here's how it applies:

Stewardship of the Body: Prioritizing overall body wellness reflects responsible stewardship of the body, recognizing it as a precious gift from God.

Self-Care and Self-Respect: Practicing good personal hygiene demonstrates self-respect and love for oneself, recognizing the body as a temple of the Holy Spirit.

Respect for Others: Maintaining personal hygiene shows consideration for others, promoting a clean and hygienic environment in shared spaces.

Community Well-Being: Being conscious of personal hygiene contributes to the well-being of the community by preventing the spread of illnesses.

Gratitude for God's Gift: Recognizing the impact of personal hygiene on overall body wellness fosters gratitude for God's gift of a healthy and functioning body.

In conclusion, understanding the holistic impact of personal hygiene on overall body wellness is vital for young men. As a young man in a Christian lifestyle, valuing overall body wellness aligns with principles of stewardship, self-care, and recognizing the body as a temple of the Holy

Spirit. By practicing good personal hygiene and caring for their bodies, young men can promote physical health, mental well-being, and self-confidence, honoring God's gift and contributing to a positive and hygienic environment for themselves and others.

Other Books by the Author

> **Whimsical Wonders:** 50 Tales of Fictional Fun

> **Love As God Intended It:** Faith, Hope, and Love, But the greatest of these is love.

> **The Bible Storybook**: 50 Exciting Stories for Kids (Volume 1)

> **The Bible Storybook:** 46 Parables: Tales of God's Kingdom and Our Lives (Volume 2)

> **The Bible Storybook**: Exploring The Transformative Power of Faith and The Miraculous Acts of Christ (Volume 3)

> **Shadows of Deception** ~The Hidden Secrets~

> **The Basilica Heist**: Shadows Unveiled

> **Vanishing Chains:** As the intricate plot continues to unfold,

> **Whispers of the Silent Shadows"** Part one

> **Beyond the Veil of Celestial Whispers:** Part Two: The Saga Continues

> **The Prophet Elisha's Unseen Paths**

> **Divine Dwelling**: Unveiling the Mysteries of the Tabernacle

> **Divine Dialogue**: Unveiling the Power of A.C.T.S in the Lord's

Author Contact Information

For information and inquiries or to see other books by the author:
Email: *Thecblogger4@gmail.com*
Or
Visit Our Website at:
www.booksbyderickchibilu.com[1]

---

1.   *http://www.booksbyderickchibilu.com*

About the Author

Derick Chibilu is an upcoming talented author and business professional based in Houston, Texas, where he resides with his beloved wife, Alice, and is known for his inspiring works. Derick holds an MBA from Capella University, a Bachelor of Business in Computer Information Systems from the University of Houston Downtown (UHD), and an Associate of Science in Business Administration from Delaware Tech.

As a born-again Christian, Derick's faith is an integral part of his life. He is an active member of the North Central Assemblies of God Church in Spring, Texas, where he finds strength and inspiration through fellowship with other believers. Derick strongly believes in God, family, and Christian family values, which are central themes in his writing.

Read more at https://www.booksbyderickchibilu.com/.